Ag and the Wind Walker

"Let's go and see Flint," said Rocky.

"Yes," said Ag. "I will take my Wind Walker."

3

"My Wind Walker will take me across the lake," said Ag.

"That is a silly idea," said Rocky.

Rotherham Library & Information Services

ge 2

ge 14

This book must be returned by the date specified at the time of issue as the DUE DATE FOR RETURN.
The loan may be extended (personally, by post, telephone or online) for a further period, if the book is not required by another reader, by quoting the barcode / author / title.

Enquiries: 01709 813034

www.rotherham.gov.uk/sls

Alison Hawes

**Story illustrated by
Pet Gotohda**

Heinemann

In this story

 Ag

 Rocky

 Flint

Tricky words

- Wind Walker
- across
- idea
- walked
- around
- there

Introduce these tricky words and help the reader when they come across them later!

Story starter

Ag and her big brother Rocky are cave people who lived long ago. Ag is full of good ideas to make their lives more comfortable, but Rocky laughs at her ideas – he's so sure they will never catch on! One day, Ag and Rocky wanted to see their friend Flint.

Rocky and Ag went to see Flint.

Rocky walked around the lake.

Ag got on her Wind Walker and went on the lake.

Rocky walked and walked.

Who do you think will get to Flint first?

The wind blew Ag's Wind Walker.

Ag went across the lake very fast.

Rocky got to Flint's cave.
There was Ag!

"How did you get here so fast?"
said Rocky.

"The wind blew my
Wind Walker," said Ag.

"It is time to go," said Ag.

"I will go on the Wind Walker," said Rocky.

The wind blew the Wind Walker.
Rocky went across the lake
very fast.

But he fell off!

"I said it was a silly idea,"
said Rocky.
"It will *never* catch on!"

Quiz

Text Detective

- What do we call 'Wind Walking' today?
- Why do you think Rocky says it is a silly idea?

Word Detective

- Phonic Focus: Blending three phonemes
  Page 3: Can you sound out 'will'?
  What is the sound in the middle?
- Page 4: Find a word that means 'foolish'.
- Page 12: Why is the word 'never' in bold print?

Super Speller

Read these words:

time   off   yes

Now try to spell them!

HA! HA! HA!

Q Where can you find a lake without water?

A On a map!

13

Find out about

- How some sports use the wind

Tricky words

- dangerous
- power
- wind-surfing
- board
- sail
- kite-surfing
- hang-gliding
- accidents

Introduce these tricky words and help the reader when they come across them later!

Text starter

Wind sports can be exciting, but they can also be dangerous. You can go very high or very far with the power of the wind.

Wind Sports

Would you try a dangerous sport?

Some dangerous sports use wind power.

Wind-surfing

Wind-surfing is a dangerous sport.

The wind-surfer stands on a board and the wind blows the sail.

The wind makes the wind-surfer go fast.
A wind-surfer went at 56mph.

Would you try wind-surfing?

Kite-surfing

Kite-surfing is a dangerous sport.

The kite-surfer stands on a board and the wind blows the kite.

Kite-surfers can do flips in the air!

The kite-surfer goes high in the air.
A kite-surfer went 15m up in the air.

Would you try kite-surfing?

Hang-gliding

Hang-gliding is a dangerous sport.

The hang-glider hangs under a sail and the wind blows the sail.

The wind makes the hang-
glider go far.
A hang-glider went 435 miles!

Would you try hang-gliding?

Lots of people like dangerous wind sports.

There are lots of accidents ...

Which wind sport would you like to try?

… but wind sports can be lots of fun!

Quiz

Text Detective

- How does wind-surfing work?
- Why do you think people do dangerous sports?

Word Detective

- **Phonic Focus:** Blending three phonemes
  Page 23: Can you sound out 'fun'?
  What is the sound in the middle?
- Page 17: Find a sentence that is a question.
- Page 17: Find a word that means the opposite of 'slow'.

Super Speller

Read these words:

under   try   far

Now try to spell them!

HA! HA! HA!

Q What colour is the wind?

A Blew!